DERRICK HENRY

NFL STAR

By Douglas Lynne

Book design by Jake Slavik
Cover design by Jake Nordby

Photographs ©: Julio Cortez/AP Images, cover, 1, 4, 6–7, 23; Gail Burton/AP Images, 9; Will Dickey/Florida Times-Union/AP Images, 10; Andrew Snook/Icon Sportswire/AP Images, 12–13; Rich Graessle/Icon Sportswire/AP Images, 15; Scott Boehm/AP Images, 16; Mark Zaleski/AP Images, 19; Perry Knotts/AP Images, 20; Red Line Editorial, 22

Press Box Books, an imprint of Press Room Editions.

Library of Congress Control Number: 2020901603

ISBN
978-1-63494-220-1 (library bound)
978-1-63494-238-6 (paperback)
978-1-63494-256-0 (epub)
978-1-63494-274-4 (hosted ebook)

Distributed by North Star Editions, Inc.
2297 Waters Drive
Mendota Heights, MN 55120
www.northstareditions.com

Printed in the United States of America
082020

ABOUT THE AUTHOR

Douglas Lynne is a freelance writer. He spent many years working in the media, first in newspapers and later for online organizations, covering everything from breaking news to politics to entertainment to sports. He lives in Minneapolis, Minnesota.

TABLE OF CONTENTS

TITANS
22
36

1

KING HENRY

The Tennessee Titans faced the Baltimore Ravens in the playoffs in January 2020. The Ravens were going to be a tough opponent. The Titans had already beaten the New England Patriots the week before. However, not many people thought they stood a chance against the Ravens. The Ravens were the top team in the conference.

Derrick Henry outruns the Ravens defense.

Henry's strength and quickness make him tough to bring down.

Early in the third quarter, the Titans got their chance to widen their lead. Running back Derrick Henry took the ball and looked

for an opening. Players from both sides were crushed together near the line of scrimmage.

Henry was light on his feet. He saw a sliver of daylight in the line. Henry used his quickness to get through the hole. A Ravens player dove to tackle him. But Henry dodged him. Then he found open field and stepped on the gas.

Ravens players tried to catch up. But Henry was too fast. He ran 66 yards before he was tackled. Henry's run set his team up for another touchdown and a 21–6 lead.

The Titans held on to win 28–12. Henry played a huge part in the victory. Every week Henry was proving himself to be one of the best backs in the National Football League (NFL).

STIFF-ARM BATTERING RAM

As a running back, several qualities make Henry a great player. He is fast and tall. But he is also heavy. His weight, combined with his speed, make Henry difficult to stop. He's also perfected the stiff-arm. He pushes defensive players out of the way so they cannot get close enough to tackle him.

Henry and a teammate celebrate the Titans' big win in Baltimore.

Riddell
2
GATORS

HIGH HOPES AND HIGH TIDE

2

Derrick Henry was born on January 4, 1994, in Yulee, Florida. He spent his childhood playing many different types of sports. Derrick's grandmother played a big role in raising Derrick. The two were very close.

In high school, Derrick was a multisport athlete. Derrick played basketball and ran on the track team. As a football player, Derrick showed he was a special talent.

Derrick set national records while playing high school football in Florida.

Derrick dives into the end zone to score a touchdown for Alabama in 2014.

He racked up 12,124 rushing yards in his high school career. That broke a 51-year-old national record. In his senior year alone, he rushed for 4,261 yards. By the time Derrick graduated, he

was ranked the top athlete in the nation and the No. 4 running back prospect for colleges.

One college that noticed Derrick's potential was Alabama. The Crimson Tide were one of the most powerful teams in college football.

They offered Derrick a football scholarship, and he accepted.

GRADUATING FOR GRANDMA

Derrick's grandmother had one wish. She wanted him to graduate from college. She knew Derrick was a talented football player. But she also recognized the importance of education. Derrick agreed with her. After he joined the Titans, he continued his college education at Alabama. Derrick graduated in 2018 with a degree in communications.

Derrick quickly began playing a big role for the Crimson Tide. He spent three seasons at Alabama. In 2015, Derrick had an outstanding season. He helped his team win the national title. That same year, Derrick was awarded the Heisman Trophy. It goes to the best player in college football. Having won a national title and Heisman Trophy, Derrick decided he was ready to enter the 2016 NFL Draft.

Derrick beams with pride after winning the Heisman Trophy.

TITANS

3

A FORCE ON HIS TEAM

The Tennessee Titans drafted Henry in the second round in 2016. In his first two seasons, he struggled to earn a starting role with the team. He was used mostly as a backup to veteran DeMarco Murray.

Then in 2018, Henry began to hit his stride. The Titans released Murray. That made Henry the starting running back. He didn't break out right away. His statistics

Henry started only four games in his first two NFL seasons.

were below average for much of the year. But in early December, he made a big splash.

In a game against the Jacksonville Jaguars, Henry rushed for 238 yards and four touchdowns. He was only the seventh player since 1970 with 200 rushing yards and four scores in a game. The next week, he proved it wasn't a fluke. He rushed for 170 yards and two more touchdowns against the New York Giants.

A RUN FOR THE RECORD BOOKS

Henry entered the NFL record books for his efforts against the Jaguars in 2018. The Titans had the ball on their own 1-yard line. Henry took a handoff and didn't stop running until he'd reached the other end zone. He became the second player in NFL history with a 99-yard touchdown run.

Henry continued to work hard. He had an even better season in 2019. And he came on strong in the second half of the schedule again. In his last six games, he rushed for

Henry outran the entire Jacksonville defense on his 99-yard touchdown.

Henry stiff-armed the Patriots into submission in the playoffs.

896 yards and 10 touchdowns. His season total of 1,540 yards earned Henry the NFL rushing title. He also tied for the NFL lead with 16 rushing touchdowns.

Henry's excellence carried over to the playoffs. He rushed for 182 yards as the Titans upset the Patriots. Then he added 195 more yards the night the Titans shocked the Ravens.

Tennessee came up one game short of the Super Bowl. The Kansas City Chiefs hosted the conference championship game. Henry scored an early touchdown and the Titans led 17–7 in the second quarter. But the Chiefs roared back. They scored four straight touchdowns and won 35–24.

Still, it had been a memorable run for Henry and the Titans. He headed into the offseason excited for their chances in 2020 and beyond.

DERRICK HENRY
2019 STATISTICS

- **Rushing:** 303 carries, 1,540 yards, 16 TDs
- **Receiving:** 18 catches, 206 yards, 2 TDs

TIMELINE MAP

1. **Yulee, Florida: 1994**
   Derrick Henry is born on January 4.
2. **Tuscaloosa, Alabama: 2013**
   Henry begins playing for the University of Alabama.
3. **New York, New York: 2015**
   Henry is awarded the Heisman Trophy.
4. **Chicago, Illinois: 2016**
   The Tennessee Titans draft Henry in the second round.
5. **Nashville, Tennessee: 2018**
   Henry scores on a 99-yard run against the Jaguars on December 6.
6. **Houston, Texas: 2019**
   Henry rushes for 211 yards against the Texans on December 29, clinching the NFL rushing title.
7. **Baltimore, Maryland: 2020**
   The Titans upset the Ravens in the playoffs on January 11, thanks in part to Henry's 195 rushing yards.

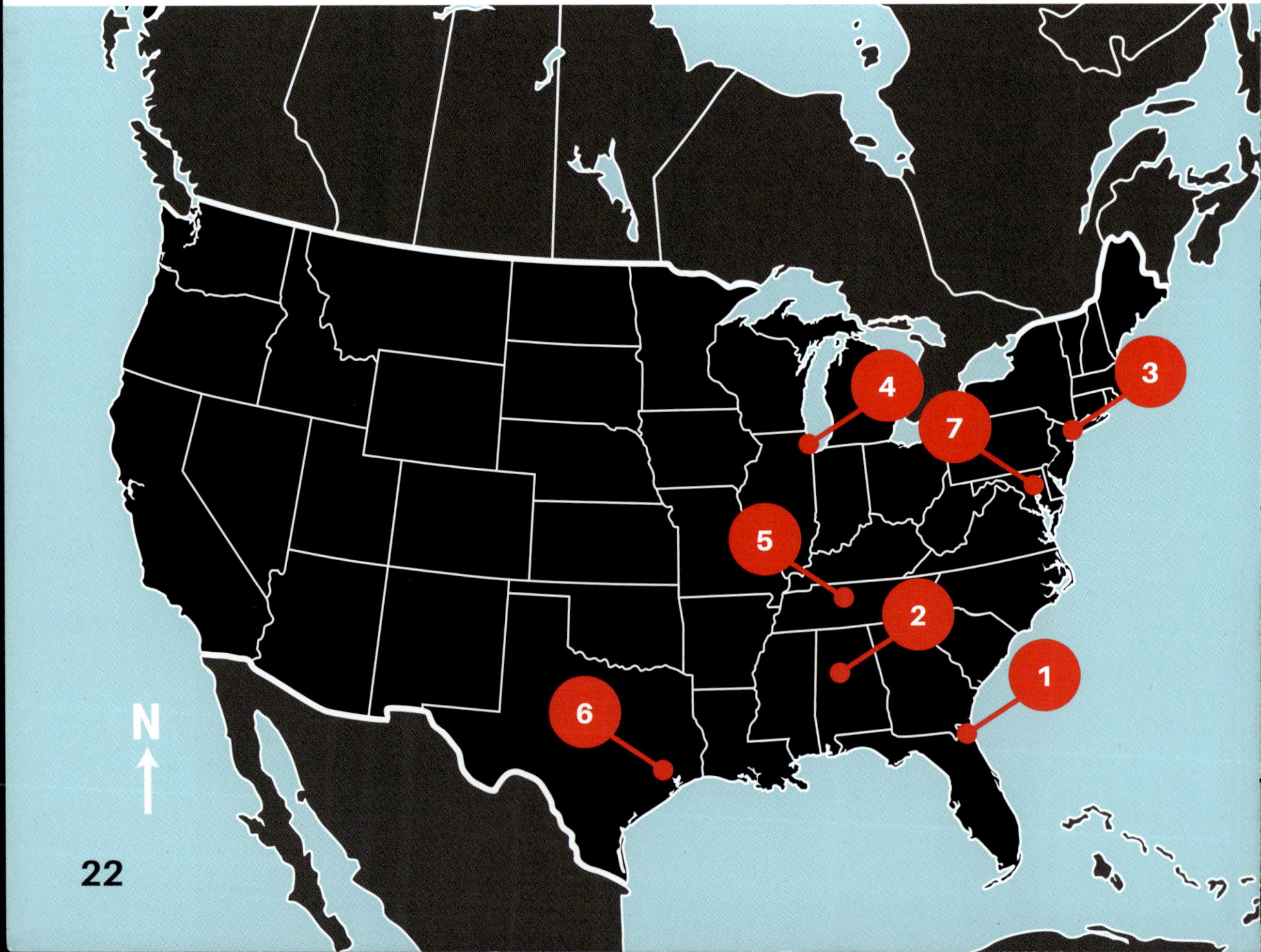

AT-A-GLANCE

DERRICK HENRY

Birth date: January 4, 1994

Birthplace: Yulee, Florida

Position: Running back

Height: 6 feet 3 inches

Weight: 247 pounds

Current team: Tennessee Titans (2016–)

Past team: Alabama Crimson Tide (2013–15)

Major awards: National High School Player of the Year (2012), Heisman Trophy (2015), AFC Offensive Player of the Month (December 2018), NFL rushing title (2019), Pro Bowl (2019)

Accurate through the 2019 season.

MORE INFORMATION

To learn more about Derrick Henry, go to **pressboxbooks.com/AllAccess**.

These links are routinely monitored and updated to provide the most current information available.

GLOSSARY

conference
A group of teams within a sports league.

draft
A system by which sports leagues divide up new talent.

fluke
An unlikely occurrence or a surprising bit of luck.

line of scrimmage
The place on the field where a play begins.

prospect
A young player who is expected to succeed.

scholarship
Money given to a student to cover college expenses, often in exchange for playing sports.

INDEX